GW01406574

All Sorts of Stuff

Ideas for activities about ourselves
for pre-key stage 1 children

by

Carole Creary and Gay Wilson

Curriculum Advisers for Primary Science

NIAS

Northamptonshire Inspection and Advisory Service

Introduction

How this book will help

It will:

- give you some understanding of how young children learn science
- provide a bank of simple and enjoyable learning activities
- build a firm foundation for later learning in science
- provide you with necessary background information
- help you to make the most of opportunities for science learning in everyday activities

What is science for the pre-school child?

With very young children, science could be defined as finding out about and making sense of the world around us and our place in it. As well as acquiring knowledge it is also about developing an enquiring and questioning attitude. Children need to be encouraged to develop their own ideas and to express these ideas in words even though at this stage the ideas may not be scientifically correct.

How do children learn science?

Science is a very practical subject and children will learn most by 'doing'. They will learn a great deal through play but this play needs to be directed if the full potential for science learning is to be realised.

They will need encouragement to use all their senses, within the bounds of safety, as they investigate and explore the world around and to talk about what they are doing and what they have found out.

- each time a child squeezes a toy they are learning about materials
- making cakes or cooking vegetables helps them realise how things may be changed by heat
- rolling out playdough or stretching fabric shows that some changes are only temporary and may easily be reversed
- everytime they play with sand or water they are discovering the properties of some everyday materials

How do we help children learn science?

- by asking questions such as;
  What do you think?
  Why do you think that?
  What if...?
- by encouraging them to question
- by encouraging them to put ideas into words
- by valuing their ideas
- by providing opportunities for children to explore using all their senses
- by helping the child to develop the appropriate language

Making the most of science

Often the opportunity to develop a child's scientific thinking is lost because the potential for science in the activity has not been recognised. Thinking clearly about why we are asking the child to do a particular activity and what is the learning we expect to take place, can be helpful. To this end we have included science learning objectives for each activity in the book.

Where next?

The activities in this book will give children a good foundation for later learning at school, including the Materials and their Properties aspect of national curriculum science.

Contents

Activity summary

This side of the page gives a summary of the children's activity to you, the adult. It gives you an idea of the sort of questions that might be raised or the way in which the children's thinking might be guided.

Objectives

This gives you the main learning that is expected from the activity. They help you plan and direct activities with greater purpose.

See it through!

I can see through the bottle but not where the label is...

- Look at the things on the table.
- Which ones can you see through?
- Hold them up and see if you can see your friend through them.
- Make a set of all the things you can see through.
- What other things can you find that you can see through?

Objectives: To know that you can see through some materials and not others.

- Make a display of transparent objects and materials.
- Invite the children to contribute.
- Introduce the words transparent and opaque if the children are ready.
- Beware! Do not use glass objects unless the children are closely supervised.

Extension:
- Introduce translucent materials and ask the children to sort into 3 sets.

You will need:
A collection of transparent and opaque objects and materials.

6

This side of the page offers you some extra help or advice and sometimes ideas for extension activities.

Beware!

This warning symbol appears wherever there may be a safety consideration. Children should be taught to work safely and sensibly. Only by encountering hazards in a safe and controlled environment will they learn to do so. More information may be found in "Be Safe!" available from the Association for Science Education, College Lane, Hatfield, Herts. AL 10 9AA. ISBN 0 86357 081 X

You will need:

This gives you a list of all the materials and equipment you will need for the activity

1

Sort it out!

> I think this is made from the same sort of stuff as this brick

> I think this stuff is called plastic

- Look at all the things very carefully.
- Do you know what they are?
- Do you know what each one is made from?
- Can you sort them into sets?

Objectives: To recognise and sort familiar materials.

- Use simple objects such as pebbles, pieces of wood or metal, small plastic objects such as bricks or yogurt pots, etc.
- Encourage the children to think of the material each object is made from rather than what the object is.

Extension:

- Introduce other objects made from the materials for the children to match and sort.

You will need:

A collection of simple objects made from wood, plastic, stone, metal, etc.

Objectives: To use the sense of touch to gather information.

To develop the appropriate language to describe various materials.

- Give the children lots of opportunities to feel and explore materials before putting them in the bag.
- Choose one to put in the bag for the children to describe.

Extension:

- Put less familiar materials in the bag without the children seeing them first.

You will need:

Feely bag, variety of materials such as playdough, stone, wood, sandpaper, fur fabric.

What does it feel like?

- What can you feel in the feely bag?
- How many words can you think of to describe what you can feel?

This stuff feels hard

sharp edges

smooth

Mine feels soft

squashy

- What do you think the stuff is?
- Try and describe what is in your bag so that your friend can guess what it is.

Rough and smooth

- Look at the things in front of you.
- Can you sort them into sets?

This feels very smooth

- Why have you put them in those sets?
- What is the same about those things in each set?
- How many different words can you think of to tell someone about them?

Objectives: To know that different materials look and feel different.
To use the senses of sight and touch to observe closely.

- Encourage the children to use their senses of sight and touch to explore the different materials and develop the appropriate language.
- When the children are familiar with the materials, hide them in a feely bag or blindfold the children, and see if they can identify them using just touch.

You will need:

A selection of rough and smooth materials, sorting rings.

Objectives: To be able to recognise shiny things.

To know that some shiny things act like mirrors.

- Make a display of shiny things and encourage the children to contribute.
- Sort objects into shiny and not-shiny sets and help the children to develop the appropriate language.
- Collect silver paper sweet wrappers for collage material.
- Use to make christmas tree baubles, robots, the sun, moon etc.

You will need:

A collection of shiny and not shiny objects for sorting.

Is it shiny?

I can see myself but I'm upside down!

- Look at all the things in front of you.
- Which are the shiny things?
- Which ones can you see yourself in?
- Can you find a really shiny thing?
- Look at yourself in it and then draw a picture of yourself.

5

See it through!

I can see through the bottle but not where the label is...

- Look at the things on the table.
- Which ones can you see through?
- Hold them up and see if you can see your friend through them.
- Make a set of all the things you can see through.
- What other things can you find that you can see through?

Objectives: To know that you can see through some materials and not others.

- Make a display of transparent objects and materials.
- Invite the children to contribute.
- Introduce the words transparent and opaque if the children are ready.

Beware!

- Do not use glass objects unless the children are closely supervised.

Extension:

- Introduce translucent materials and ask the children to sort into 3 sets.

You will need:

A collection of transparent and opaque objects and materials.

6

Objectives: To understand that there are many different types of paper.
To use simple tools such as scissors and glue spreaders.

· Discuss the properties of the different papers with the children.
· Make a display of things made from paper or card.
· Children could make individual pictures or the different papers could be used to make a large group or class collage.

You will need:

Paper or card in a variety of weights, colours and textures, scissors, glue, spreaders, crayons.

Paper chase

This feels all bumpy

This has got writing all over it

· How many different sorts of paper can you find?
· How many ways could you sort them?
· Which one would you like to draw a picture on? Why?
· Tear or cut some of the other papers into pieces and stick them on your picture to make it more interesting.

7

Changing shape

Look at and feel your playdough.

How many different ways can you change its shape?

Does it keep its new shape?

What happens if you push your finger into the playdough?

Can you make a long thin shape?

Can you make a flat shape?

Objectives: To know that you can change the shape of some materials.

Playdough

2 cups plain flour,   1 cup salt,

2 cups water,   2 tblsps cooking oil,

2 tsps cream of tartar, food colouring

Mix a few drops of food colouring with the water and then mix all the ingredients together in a large saucepan. Cook over a moderate heat, stirring constantly until the mixture forms a ball. Allow to cool a little and knead into a smooth ball.

You will need:

Playdough, rolling pin, pastry cutters etc.

Objectives: To know that water can be frozen to make ice.

To know that ice melts to form water.

· You will need to make the ice cubes with the children the day before doing the melting activity.

· Use food colouring and make the colour fairly strong so that it can be seen clearly as the ice begins to melt.

· Discuss what is happening as the ice melts.

· Be careful not to disturb the bowl.

· Encourage the appropriate language, eg melt, mix, cold, frozen, freeze, ice, etc.

You will need:

Water, food colouring, ice-cube trays, access to a freezer, clear bowl or tank.

Coloured ice

The ice is floating

I can see coloured bits floating away

· Look at the coloured ice cubes.

· What do they feel like?

· What happens as they begin to get warm?

· Put some into a bowl of water.

· Watch carefully – Don't touch!

· What is happening to the ice?

· Where has it gone?

9

What does water do?

The water makes this wheel go round.

I can't fill this sieve up!

- What does water feel like?
- What happens to the water wheel when you pour water on it?
- What happens when you stop?
- Can you catch some water in a sieve?
- How many things can you think of that we use water for?

Objectives: To experience and begin to understand some of the ways in which water behaves.

- Encourage the children to observe closely what is happening as they play with the water.
- Use the appropriate language, eg wet, drop, dribble, splash, pour, full, empty, etc.

Extension:

- Compare the way water and dry sand behave using the same equipment.
- What is the same about them?
- What is different?

You will need:

A water trough or large bowl, toy water wheel, sieve, jugs, other suitable containers.

Objectives: To explore the properties of wet and dry sand.

- Use fine silver sand if possible.
- Encourage the children to talk about what the sand feels like.
- Look at some sand under a good magnifier to see what it is made from.
- If possible have two sand trays when comparing wet and dry sand.
- Encourage the children to try doing the same things with both types of sand to compare the behaviour of the two materials.

You will need:
Various containers, spoons, spades, 'water' wheel.

In the sand pit

- What does dry sand feel like?
- How is wet sand different?
- Which one is best for making sand pies? Why?

This sand makes good pies

This makes the wheel go round

- Can you make a tunnel for your car to go through?
- Which sand is best for making the wheel go round?
- Which will make the highest pile?

Wash day

- Collect up the dolls' dirty clothes.
- How could you get them clean?

If you put soap in you get lots of bubbles

Do I just put them in or do I have to rub them?

- Do you need soap powder?
- Do the clothes come cleaner if you use warm water?
- How could you find out?

Objectives: To begin to think about fair testing.

Beware! · Some children may react adversely to detergents.

Encourage the children to give their ideas of how they could find out whether it is better to wash clothes with or without soap powder or detergent.

- Use two bowls of cold water · put soap in one and not the other.
- Wash similar clothes in each bowl and compare the results.
- Repeat using warm water.

You will need:

2 bowls, dolls clothes (dirty), soap powder or detergent, water, clothes line, pegs.

Objectives: To know that some fabrics dry faster than others.

To practise making predictions.

- Use two very different fabrics to begin with, eg cotton and wool.
- Encourage the children to feel and talk about the different fabrics.
- Help to develop the appropriate language.
- Talk about why one fabric dried quicker.
- Was it the one expected to be best?

Extension:
- Try with a wider range of fabrics.

You will need:
Similar squares of fabric, a bowl, water, washing line and pegs.

Which dries quickest?

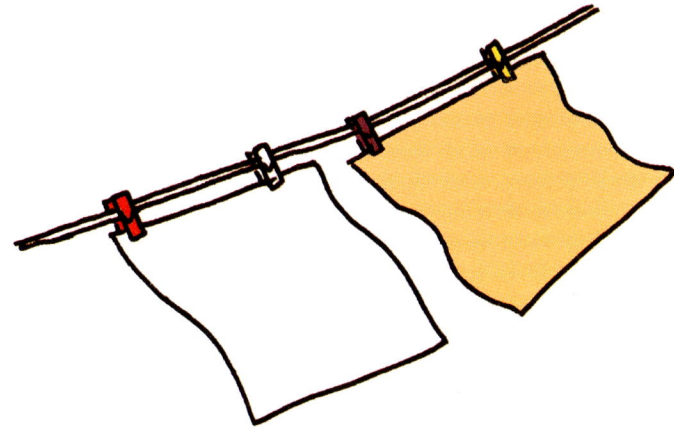

- Feel the two fabrics.
- Use a magnifier to look more closely.
- Make them both really wet.
- Hang them on the line to dry.
- Which one do you think will dry first?
- Why do you think that?
- What do you think would help to make them dry quicker?

Keeping Teddy dry

- Teddy is getting wet!
- Can you find some material that will make him a rain hat?
- Make sure the water won't go through the material.
- What could Teddy put on his feet?
- What else would he need to keep him dry?

Objectives: To know that some materials will not let water through.

- Have a range of materials including some waterproof fabrics and plastic sheeting.
- Make sure children are not left unsupervised with plastic bags or sheeting.

Beware!

- Test the fabrics by stretching them over a container and pouring water on to them.
- See if the little figure gets wet!

You will need:

A range of materials, a clear container, a small figure, elastic bands, jug, water.

Objectives: To know that some materials are better than others for keeping us warm.

- Encourage the children to feel a wide variety of fabrics.
- Help them to develop the appropriate language to describe the material eg thick, thin, woolly, fluffy, thin, silky, etc.
- Talk about the sort of clothes that might be made from each fabric.
- Make a display of clothes suitable for hot or cold weather.

You will need:

Pieces of fabric, a Teddy bear or doll, a range of clothes to fit.

Keeping Teddy warm

- Look at Teddy's clothes.
- Which do you think would keep him warm on a cold day?
- Dress Teddy in the warmest clothes.
- Which material would be the best for making him a summer outfit?

Stone pudding

Take 2 cups of sand

2 cups of fine gravel

some small stones

Mix them altogether.

It's quite hard to mix

I know that sand will go through the sieve but I'm not sure about the gravel

- What does your mixture look like?
- Can you still see the different ingredients?
- How could you sort them out again?

Objectives: To have experience in sorting and sieving mixtures.
To know that some changes may be reversed.

- Encourage the children to make the mixture themselves so that they see the original ingredients.
- The stones may be sorted by hand but provide sieves of different mesh size for the children to investigate.

Extension:

- Compare this mixture with a cake mixture.
- Add metal objects to the mixture that may be sorted using a magnet.

You will need:

Sand, gravel, stones or beads, sieves, mixing bowls, large spoon, measuring cup.

Objectives: To know that some things will dissolve in water.

- Sugar or salt may be used for this activity.
- Encourage the children to talk about what is happening.
- The children may not understand the term 'dissolve' and may wish to use 'disappear' at this stage.
- To find out if the sugar is still there, the children could taste the solution but make sure that conditions are hygienic.

You will need:

Water, sugar or salt, small plastic containers, spoons.

Where has it gone?

I could see the sugar when I first put it in.

When I stir it, it all goes round but it seems to be disappearing!

- Put a spoonful of sugar into some water.
- Look carefully. What can you see?
- What do you think will happen if you stir it?
- Stir it and find out.
- Where do you think the sugar has gone?
- How could you find out?

Wiggly Woo

- Look at all the materials.
- What can you say about them?
- Which ones could you use to make a wiggly worm?

This ribbon makes a good worm but the lolly sticks don't!

- Why can't you make wiggly worms from all the materials?
- How many words can you think of to describe the materials?

Objectives: To find out that some materials are flexible while others are not.

- Allow the children to handle all the materials and describe them using the appropriate language.
- A large stand magnifier is useful for looking more closely at the materials.
- At this stage make sure the materials offered to the children are either quite flexible or really rigid. So that they may distinguish easily between them.
- Add less rigid or bendy materials as an extension activity.

You will need:

A collection of materials including fabric, ribbon, lolly sticks, wool, matchsticks, teaspoon, pencil, shoelace, etc.

Objectives: To find out which type of thread is best for sewing.

To practise hand/eye co-ordination.

- Use commercial sewing cards or make simple ones by punching holes in stiff card.
- Loose weave tapestry canvas may also be useful for 'more experienced' sewers.
- Provide different thicknesses of thread, eg thick and thin wool, cotton, smooth string, hairy string, shoe or threading laces.
- Use only blunt bodkins, if these are necessary, and only under supervision.

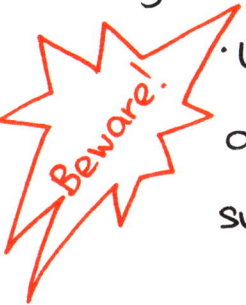

Beware!

You will need:
Sewing cards or coarse canvas, various types of thread.

Sew it up!

I've seen my Mum sewing things

She sews buttons on like this but she also has a sewing machine.

- Choose a sewing card and some thread.
- Sew carefully in and out of the holes to make a pattern.
- Can you use more than one thread?
- Which thread is easiest to use? Why?
- Can you sew two cards together?
- Can you find some other things that are sewn together?

Stretching it!

This material stretches quite a lot

That's funny, When I stretch it, it gets thinner!

- Feel the materials in front of you.
- Which ones do you think will stretch?
- Put them together into a set.
- Now try them - did you choose the right ones?
- Can you think of some other things that stretch?
- What could you use them for?

Objectives: To understand the word 'stretchy'. To know that some materials will stretch while others will not.

- Children could be encouraged to work with a partner for this activity.
- Choose materials that are really stretchy or don't stretch at all so that the children can distinguish easily between them.

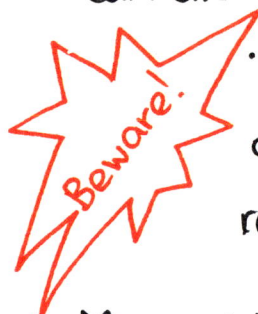

Beware!

- Do not use thin elastic bands which can be dangerous when stretched and released.
- More able children may find out which is the stretchiest material.

You will need:

Various materials such as lollysticks, velvet, paper, string, tights, jersey, thick rubber band, knitted fabric.

Objectives: To know that some things are attracted to a magnet.

- Discuss with the children which things they think will be attracted to the magnet.
- Encourage them to develop their ideas about why this might happen.
- At this stage, make sure that all the metal objects used are attracted to the magnet. Add non-magnetic metals as an extension.

Beware!

- Beware of small metal objects which may be swallowed.

You will need:
Magnets, a collection of magnetic and non-magnetic objects.

What does a magnet do?

- Look carefully at all the things you have been given.
- Which ones do you think the magnet will pick up?
- Sort them into sets.
- Now test them with your magnet.
- Which ones did the magnet pick up?
- What do you notice about all the things the magnet picked up?

Vegetable soup 1

- Look at all the vegetables.
- What colour are they?
- What shape are they?
- What do they feel like?

- What do they look like inside?
- Which ones have the same pattern inside?
- What do they smell like?
- What do they taste like?
- Can you hear them crunch when you eat them?

Objectives: To develop skills of observation.
To observe similarities and differences between vegetables.

- Encourage children to use all their senses.
- Allow children to taste the vegetables only if conditions are hygienic.
- Children should be trained to use a knife safely. Blunt knives are inappropriate for this task and may be more dangerous than a reasonably sharp one.

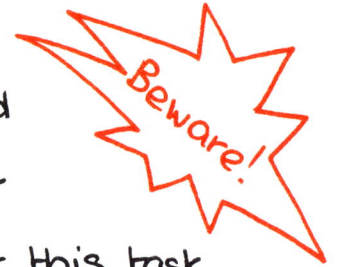

Beware!

- An adult should cut the vegetables for close observation and then into manageable pieces for the children to cut into small pieces for the soup.

You will need:

A good selection of vegetables, reasonably sharp knives, chopping board, magnifiers.

Objectives: To practise observational skills.

To experience how vegetables change when cooked.

Beware!

· Make sure that all safety precautions are taken while making the soup.

· The addition of vegetable stock cubes adds flavour to the soup without compromising religious or ethical beliefs.

· Keep a few raw pieces of each vegetable so that they can be compared with the cooked ones.

· Make sure the soup has cooled before eating.

You will need:

Chopped raw vegetables, a large saucepan, stock cubes, wooden spoon, cups or bowls and spoons, hand lens.

Vegetable soup 2

· Carefully chop the vegetables into small pieces.

· Save a piece of each one.

· Put the rest into a saucepan with water to cover them.

· Ask an adult to put the pan on the cooker and cook the soup.

This tastes good!

This smells good!

· When it is cooled, look at the vegetables - can you find the ones you put in?

· How have they changed?

Fairy cakes.

· Look at all the ingredients you are going to use to make your cakes.

The flour is soft and white...

..that feels greasy

The eggs go all bubbly when you mix them.

· Mix the ingredients together to make your cakes.

· What is the mixture like now?

· How do you think it will change when it is cooked?

Objectives: To make fairy cakes.

To investigate the different textures of baking ingredients.

To experience how materials change when cooked.

Fairy cake recipe:

100gms margarine,   2 eggs, 100gms sugar, 100gms S.R. flour,   18 paper cases.

· Cream the margarine and sugar and add the lightly beaten eggs. Fold in the sifted flour.

· Divide between the paper cases and bake in a moderate oven until golden brown.

· Use this opportunity to practise rules of hygiene.

You will need:

Ingredients as per recipe, mixing bowls, scales, mixing spoons, teaspoons, paper cases, access to oven, baking tray.

Objectives: To know that nails can be hammered into wood.

To experience using tools.

To have fun!

Beware!

- Children using tools should always be closely supervised.
- Children could use different coloured wool or ribbon to weave between the nails to finish their work.

Extension:

- Use nails to fix wheels to a block to make a simple vehicle.

You will need:

Blocks of soft wood, large nails, hammer, ribbon or wool.

Peter hammers with one hammer!

I must be very careful with my hammer

- Use the hammer carefully to hammer nails into your block of wood.
- What does it feel like?
- How hard do you have to hit the nail?
- Do you think you could push the nail into the wood without the hammer?
- Knock lots of nails into the wood to make a pattern.

25

Traditional Rhymes

Baa! Baa! Black Sheep

Pat-a-cake

Lucy Locket

Humpty Dumpty

Songs

The wise man & the foolish man
    Okki-Tokki-Unga A & C Black   ISBN 0 7136 4078 2

There's a hole in my bucket
One potato
    Apusskidu A & C Black   ISBN 0 7136 1553 2

Wiggly woo
    Sing a Song 1 *(out of print but many schools already have this book)*
    Nelson   ISBN 01741 3002 3

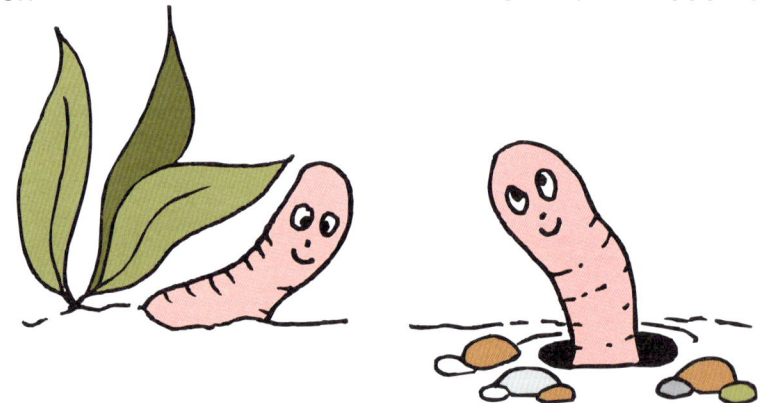

Stories

Stories are often a good way of introducing science activities. Below are a few suggestions of stories that will help introduce or reinforce work on materials.

Mrs Mopple's washing line
    Anita Hewitt
    Picture Puffin   ISBN 0 14 050028 6

The mice who lived in a shoe
    Rodney Peppe
    Picture Puffin   ISBN 0 14 050413 3

The house on the rock
    Nick Butterworth & Mick Inkpen
    Marshall Morgan & Scott   ISBN 0 551 01279 X

Five minutes peace
    Jill Murphy
    Picture puffin   ISBN 0 7445 0918 1

Three little pigs
    Ladybird   ISBN 0 7214 9527 3

Materials - essential background knowledge

Collecting materials

It is useful to have collections of different materials which children can use for sorting and grouping. Collections may take different forms:

- a collection of different objects made from similar materials
- a collection of similar objects made from different materials

Through handling a wide range of materials children will be helped to enrich their vocabulary and begin to describe similarities and differences.

Sorting and grouping

Children need a great deal of experience of sorting and grouping objects and materials in order to lay the foundations for later work in classification. They need to be given many opportunities for developing their skills of observation using all their appropriate senses. At first they will sort to given criteria, later progressing to choosing their own criteria.

To begin with children may sort according to the attributes of the objects such as colour or shape rather than the properties of the material such as rough, smooth, transparent, etc. They need to be encouraged to think about the simple properties through questions such as:

- What does it feel like?
- Can you bend it?
- Can you see through it?
- Can you squash it?

By investigating the properties of materials children should begin to understand why materials are chosen for a particular purpose:

- glass for windows
- fabrics for clothes
- plastic for buckets

Changing materials

Materials can be changed in different ways. Some of these changes may be temporary (later called physical change) and others permanent (later called chemical change). Squashing, bending, stretching, cutting and mixing some materials are examples of temporary changes while cooking, burning or firing clay are examples of permanent changes. Questions such as

- Can you get the raw vegetables back from the soup?
- Can you get the flour out of the cake?
- Can you roll your playdough out again?

will help the children to begin to appreciate the difference between these changes.